KU-586-628

Maths
Keywords

NUMBERS AND CALCULATIONS

Karen Bryant-Mole

WAYLAND

Titles in the series

English Keywords – Words and Sentences

Maths Keywords – Numbers and Calculations

Science Keywords – The Living World

Science Keywords – The Material World

670674

MORAY COUNCIL
Department of Technical
& Leisure Services

J510.3

All Wayland books encourage children to read and help them improve their literacy.

✓ The contents page, page numbers, headings and index help children find specific pieces of information.

✓ The layout of the book helps children understand and use alphabetically ordered texts.

✓ The design of the book helps children scan text to locate particular key words.

✓ The structure of the book helps children understand and use non-fiction texts that are made up of definitions and explanations.

If a particular key word has an unusual plural form or appears in a modified form within the text of the book, this form has been shown in brackets.

Design: Jean Wheeler
Cover design: Viccari Wheele
Consultant: Janet Tomlinson

First published in 1999 by Wayland Publishers Limited, 61 Western Road, Hove, East Sussex BN3 1JD

© Copyright 1999 BryantMole Books

British Library Cataloguing in Publication Data

Bryant-Mole, Karen
Maths Keywords – Numbers and Calculations.-
(Keywords)
1. Mathematics – Juvenile literature
I. Title
510.3

ISBN 07502 2418 5

Printed and bound by Eurographica S.p.a. - Marano

Acknowledgements
The publishers would like to thank the following for allowing their pictures to be reproduced in this book.
(t) = top (b) = bottom
Zul Mukhida: 4(b); 5(b); 6(t); 7(b); 9(t); 11(both); 12(t); 14(t); 15(t); 16(both); 18(t); 20(middle); 21(all); 22(t); 23(t); 24(b); 25(all); 26(t); 27(t); 28(b); 29(b); 30(b); 31(both)
Positive Images: 13(b); 17(b)
Tony Stone Images: 4(t) Donna Day; 6(b) Dan Smith; 9(b) Robert E Daemmrich; 12(b) Frans Lanting; 15(b) Ian O'Leary; 19(t) Hubert Camille; 19(b) David Joel; 20(t) Simeone Huber; 22(b); 23(b) Geoff Franklin; 27(b) Frans Lanting; 28(t) Alan Thornton; 29(t) Jon Gray; 30(b) Ian Shaw
Wayland Publishers Limited: 13(t); 14(b)
Steve Wheele: 5(t); 7(t); 8(both); 10(both); 17(t); 18(b); 24(t); 26(b)

Contents

How to use this book

This book is made up of key words. Each key word is printed in **bold** and is followed by an explanation.

• The key words are listed in alphabetical order. The words printed in large letters at the top of the page will help you find the key word you are looking for. The word at the top of each left-hand page is the first key word that appears on that page. The word at the top of each right-hand page is the last key word that appears on that page. Every key word that comes in between those words can also be found on these two pages.

• You will find an index in the back of the book. The index will show you where the explanation of each key word can be found, other pages where that word appears and where you can find any related pictures.

• As you read through an explanation, you will notice that some of the words may be underlined. Each of these underlined words has its own explanation.

Enjoy exploring the Keywords trail!

add

a

add Put together with. The symbol + is used to mean add. So, 6+3 means 6 put together with 3. (See also addition and plus.)

addition A number operation that involves adding two or more numbers. The order in which the numbers are added does not change the answer. 4+5=9 and 5+4=9.
Addition is the inverse of subtraction. If 5-3=2, then 2+3=5. (See also plus and sum.)

approximate Give a rough answer. (See also approximately and exact.)

approximately Roughly. The symbol ≈ or ≃ means 'is approximately equal to'. So, 29+9≈40 means 29 plus 9 is approximately equal to 40.

arithmetic To do with using numbers. It includes counting and operations such as addition, subtraction, multiplication and division.

array An arrangement of dots in columns and rows.

ascending order Going up in order of size from the smallest to the biggest. The numbers 4, 7, 3, 9 and 2, written in ascending order, are 2, 3, 4, 7, 9.

▲ This little boy is **adding** an egg to the mixture in the bowl.

▲ Going from the smallest to the biggest is called **ascending order**.

associative To do with the fact that the order in which three or more numbers are added or multiplied does not change the answer. For example, 4+3+2, 4+2+3, 3+2+4, 3+4+2, 2+4+3 and 2+3+4 all make 9.

b

$$\begin{array}{r} 47 \\ +\ 36 \\ \hline {\scriptstyle 1} \\ 83 \end{array}$$

▲ Adding 7 and 6 crosses the tens **boundary**.

boundary (boundaries) Where one thing ends and another begins. It is sometimes used to describe the change-over point between places. Adding 7 and 6, which are both units, would cross the tens boundary because the answer, which is 13, is made up of one ten and three units.

brackets Symbols which are used to group things together. Brackets are used to show the order in which operations should be done. It is important to do the operation inside the brackets first. For example, 7-(3+2)=7-5=2. Doing the operations in a different order will give you a different answer.

c

calculate Work out.

calculation Something that has to be worked out. Sometimes called a problem.

▲ A calculator can help you do **calculations**.

cancel

cancel Make a fraction smaller and easier to work with by dividing both the numerator and the denominator by the same number. $\frac{9}{12}$ can be cancelled to $\frac{3}{4}$. Both the numerator and the denominator have been divided by 3. (See also lowest terms.)

cardinal number Any number that describes how many. 1, 57 and 165 are all cardinal numbers.

carry To do with numbers crossing boundaries in number operations. When 47+36 is written in columns, the 7 and the 6 are added first, giving 13. The 1 ten is then carried over into the tens column.

classify Sort into a named group. 6, for example, can be classified as an even number.

column A line that goes from top to bottom, rather than from side to side. When number operations are written with one number below another, they are said to be set out in columns. (See also row.)

common denominator When two or more fractions have the same denominator, it is called a common denominator. $\frac{3}{16}$ and $\frac{7}{16}$ have a common denominator. Fractions with different denominators

▲ This girl is seven years old. Seven is a **cardinal number**.

▲ These parachutists have formed a **column**.

can be changed into fractions with a common denominator by making one or both into an equivalent fraction. The fractions ¼ and ⅛ have different denominators. However, if ¼ is changed into the equivalent fraction ²⁄₈, both fractions will have a common denominator.

Fractions must have a common denominator before they can be added or subtracted. ²⁄₈+⅛=³⁄₈. ²⁄₈-⅛=⅛. (See also lowest common denominator.)

common factor A number that is a factor of two or more numbers.
The factors of 10 are 1, 2, 5 and 10.
The factors of 12 are 1, 2, 3, 4, 6 and 12. So, the common factors of 10 and 12 are 1 and 2.
2 is called the highest common factor or the greatest common factor of 10 and 12, as it is the highest factor that both numbers have.

common multiple A number that is a multiple of two or more numbers.
3, 6, 9, 12 and 15 are all multiples of 3. 5, 10 and 15 are multiples of 5. So, 15 is a common multiple of 3 and 5. It can be called the least, or lowest, common multiple of 3 and 5 as it is the lowest multiple that both numbers have.

factors of 10

factors of 12

▲ The **common factors** of ten and twelve are 1 and 2.

▲ 15 is a **common multiple** of 3 and 5.

commutative

commutative To do with the fact that the order in which two or more numbers are added or multiplied does not change the answer. 3+4 and 4+3 both make 7. 3x4 and 4x3 both make 12.

compare (comparing) Find out if two things are the same or different.

compensation A method of addition or subtraction. In addition, a rounded number that is more than the number you need to add is added and then the difference between the rounded number and the actual number is taken away. In subtraction, a rounded number that is more than the number is taken away and the difference is then added. (See also complementary addition and decomposition.)

complementary addition A method of subtraction. The answer is worked out by finding how many have to be added to the second number to get to the first number. Think of 34-16 as adding 4 to the 16 to get to 20, adding 10 to the 20 to get to 30 and adding 4 to the 30 to get to 34. 4+10+4=18, so 34-16=18. (See also compensation and decomposition.)

composite number Any number that is not a prime number. Composite numbers have more factors than just themselves and 1. 6 is a composite number as it has four factors: 1, 2, 3 and 6.

$$76 - 60 = 16$$
$$16 + 1 = 17$$

$$\begin{array}{r} 76 \\ - 59 \\ \hline 17 \end{array}$$

▲ This method of subtraction is called **compensation**.

$$16 + 4 = 20$$
$$20 + 10 = 30$$
$$30 + 4 = 34$$
$$4 + 10 + 4 = 18$$

$$\begin{array}{r} 34 \\ - 16 \\ \hline 18 \end{array}$$

▲ This method of subtraction is called **complementary addition**.

consecutive Follow on, without any gaps. The numbers 53, 54, 55, 56 and 57, for example, are consecutive numbers.

conservation To do with the fact that the total number of objects in a set is not changed by moving them around or counting them in a different order.

continue Carry on, in the same way.

count Say number names in order. To count how many, start at 1 and give each object a number name. The last number you say tells you how many there are altogether.

cube To find the cube of a number, you multiply it by itself and then multiply it by itself again. 4x4x4=64, so 64 is 4 cubed. It can be written as 4^3. A number, such as 64, that is another number cubed is called a cubic number.

d

decimal To do with a pattern of counting that is based on ten. It often means a number that includes a decimal fraction, such as 54·376 or 0·02. (See also decimal place and decimal point.)

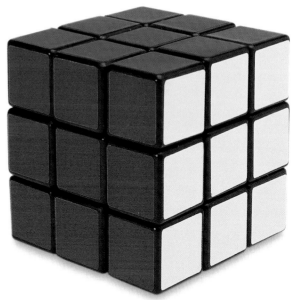

▲ 3 **cubed** is 27.

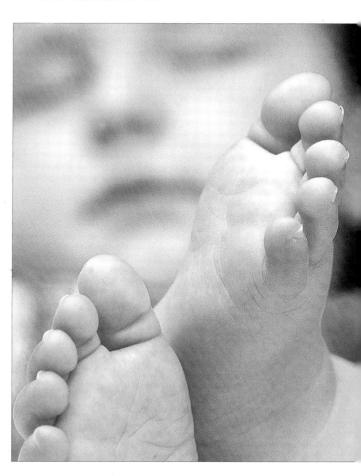

▲ The **decimal** system is based on ten.

decimal fraction

decimal fraction A fraction that is shown after a decimal point. 0·3, 0·62 and 0·837 are all decimal fractions. (See also decimal place.)

$$8 \qquad \frac{4}{10} \qquad \frac{9}{100} \qquad \frac{2}{1000}$$

decimal place To do with the place value of decimal fractions. The first place after the decimal point shows tenths, the second shows hundredths, the third shows thousandths and so on. The number 8·492 means 8 units, 4 tenths, 9 hundredths and 2 thousandths.

8 · 4 9 2

▲ Different **decimal places** have different values.

decimal point A dot that is used to separate a whole number from a decimal fraction.

decomposition A written method of subtraction that is done by regrouping. To find out what 53-27 is, 27 is written underneath 53. 7 cannot be taken from 3, so one of the 5 tens is exchanged for ten units, which are added to the 3, making 13. The 7 is then subtracted from 13 and the 2 tens are subtracted from the 4 tens that are left. (See also compensation and complementary addition.)

decrease Get smaller or make smaller.

denominator The number written below the line in a fraction. In the fraction ¾, the denominator is 4. It shows how many equal parts the whole is made up of. (See also numerator.)

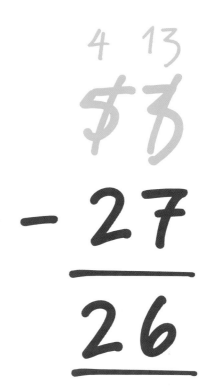

▲ This method of subtraction is called **decomposition**.

divisible by

derive Work out from something that is already known.

descending order Going down in order of size from the biggest to the smallest. The numbers 4, 7, 3, 9 and 2, written in descending order, are 9, 7, 4, 3, 2.

difference The amount by which one number is greater or less than another.

digit Also called a figure. Any one of the numerals 0, 1, 2, 3, 4, 5, 6, 7, 8 and 9. Numbers can be made up of one or many digits. 3 is a one-digit, or single-digit, number; 12 is a two-digit number; 385 is a three-digit number; 1 000 000 000 is a 10-digit number.

distributive To do with being able to spread out a multiplication calculation. 24x6 is the same as (20+4)x6, which is the same as (20x6)+(4x6) which is 120+24, which equals 144.

divide (dividing) Share. The symbol for 'divide by' is ÷. (See also division.)

divisible by Can be divided by. One number is divisible by another number if it can be divided exactly by that number without leaving a remainder. 12 is divisible by 4 because it can be divided by 4 exactly 3 times. A number is divisible by any of its factors. (See also division.)

▲ Going from the biggest to the smallest is called **descending order**.

▲ Each of these numerals is a **digit**.

division

division A number operation.
Division can be thought of as either
grouping or sharing.
12÷3, can be thought of as finding out
how many groups of three you can get
from 12. If you had 12 objects and took
out groups of 3 objects, you would have
4 groups, so there are 4 groups of 3 in
12. It is like thinking of division as
repeated subtraction. 12-3=9, 9-3=6,
6-3=3 and 3-3=0.
The same operation can be thought of
as sharing out 12 objects equally
between 3 people. Each person would
get 4 objects.
Division is the inverse of multiplication.
5x3=15, so 15÷3=5. (See also fraction,
quotient and remainder.)

divisor In the division operation 12÷3, the
divisor is 3. It can be thought of as the
number that 12 is to be divided by or
the number that is divided into 12.

double (doubling) Make two times, or
twice, the size. If you double 4, you get
8. You can think of it as 4 plus 4 or 4
multiplied by 2.
Double is the inverse of halve.

equal The same size or amount.

▲ These sandwiches have been
shared out. **Division** can be
thought of as sharing.

▲ The reflection **doubles** the
number of elephants you
can see.

equals Is the same as, or 'makes'. The symbol for equals is =. (See also equation.)

equation A number sentence that includes the equals symbol. Everything on one side of the symbol has the same value as everything on the other side, for example 4+5=9, or 7+5=6+6.

equivalent Has an equal value, or means the same amount, but may be written in a different form. The proper fraction ½ and the decimal fraction 0·5 are equivalent because they both mean a half. (See also equivalent fractions.)

equivalent fractions Fractions that mean the same amount. ½, ⁴⁄₈ and ⁵⁄₁₀ are equivalent fractions. They all mean a half.
A fraction can be changed to an equivalent fraction by multiplying or dividing both the numerator and the denominator by the same amount. ³⁄₆ is equivalent to ½. The numerator and the denominator have both been divided by 3.

estimate (estimating) Use rounded numbers to give an answer that is roughly correct but may not be exact. Can also be used to mean make a reasonable, or sensible, guess. (See also approximate.)

▲ A fraction wall helps you work out **equivalent fractions**.

▲ This man has to **estimate** how long the ship's journey will take.

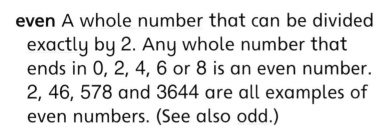

even A whole number that can be divided exactly by 2. Any whole number that ends in 0, 2, 4, 6 or 8 is an even number. 2, 46, 578 and 3644 are all examples of even numbers. (See also odd.)

exact Completely correct. An exact answer has not been estimated or approximated. An exact number has not been rounded.

exactly Completely. A number that is divisible by another number exactly has no part left over. 12 can be divided by 3 exactly four times.

exchange Change for something that has the same value. For example, 1 ten can be exchanged for 10 units.

expanded form A number or number sentence written in a longer form. 4000+500+20+7, for example, is an expanded form of 4527.

express Show in a particular form. 50%, for instance, is half expressed as a percentage.

f

fact Something that is true.

factor A number that can be divided into another number exactly. 1, 2, 3, 4,

▲ 8 is an **even** number.

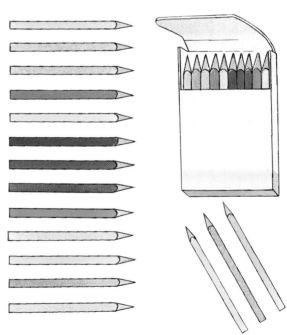

▲ 13 crayons can be **exchanged** for one packet of 10 crayons and 3 single crayons.

6 and 12 can all be divided into 12 exactly, so 12 has six factors. (See also common factor and prime factor.)

factorise Make a number simpler by splitting it into its factors.

fewer Not as many.

figure Another word for digit.

formula A rule, often shown as an equation.

fraction A part of something. Fractions can be shown as decimal fractions and percentages but the word fraction is often used to mean a number written as a numerator over a denominator, such as ⅜. The bottom number shows how many equal parts the whole thing is made up of. The top number shows how many parts we are dealing with. If one whole pizza is cut into four equal parts, one piece is written as ¼ because it is 1 of 4 equal parts. All the pieces together can be written as 4/4 because we are dealing with 4 of 4 equal parts. 4/4 is the same as one whole, or 1. Fractions are linked to division. Cutting one pizza into four equal pieces is the same as dividing it into four pieces, or dividing it by four. So, ¼ can also be thought of as 1÷4. (See also equivalent fraction, improper fraction, mixed number and proper fraction.)

▲ There are **fewer** forks than knives.

▲ This slice of pizza is a **fraction** of the whole pizza.

greater

g

greater Larger, or bigger. 10 is said to be greater than 5 because it means a larger amount. ½ is greater than ¼ because it means a larger part of something. 'Greater than' is shown by the symbol >. 'Greater than or equal to' is shown by the symbol ≥. (See also less.)

group Put things together, often because they belong together. (See also regroup.)

h

half One of two equal parts. It is a fraction. It is written as ½ when expressed as a proper fraction. It is written as 50% when expressed as a percentage and 0·5 when expressed as a decimal fraction. Two halves make one whole.

halve (halving) Make half the size. It is the inverse of double. To double a number you can multiply it by 2. To halve a number you divide it by 2.

highest common factor (See common factor.)

hundred Ten tens. It is written as 100. The place where the 1 is, is called the hundreds place. If something is divided into one hundred equal parts, each part is called a hundredth.

▲ **Half** this clown's hat is green. The other **half** is red.

▲ There are one **hundred** squares marked on this board game.

i

improper fraction A fraction with a numerator that is greater than the denominator, such as ⁴⁄₃. Also called a top-heavy fraction. Improper fractions can be changed to mixed numbers or whole numbers. ⁴⁄₃ is the same as 1⅓, because ³⁄₃ equals one whole and there is ⅓ left over. (See also proper fraction.)

increase Get bigger or make bigger.

integer A positive or negative whole number.

inverse To do with undoing, or reversing, something that has been done. Addition and subtraction are the inverse of each other. If 2 and 7 are added, the answer is 9. If 7 is then subtracted from 9, the addition is undone and the answer is goes back to 2. Multiplication and division are the inverse of each other. If 4 is multiplied by 2, the answer is 8. If 8 is then divided by 2 the answer goes back to 4. Doubling and halving are the inverse of each other.

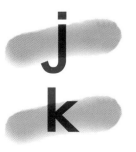

j

k

$$\frac{4}{3} = \frac{3}{3} + \frac{1}{3}$$

$$\frac{4}{3} = 1\frac{1}{3}$$

▲ ⁴⁄₃ is an **improper fraction**.

▲ The route number on this tram can be called an **integer**.

less

l

less Smaller. 5 is said to be less than 10 because it means a smaller amount.
¼ is less than ½ because it means a smaller part of something. 'Less than' is shown by the symbol <. 'Less than or equal to' is shown by the symbol ≤. (See also greater.)

lowest common denominator The lowest number that a set of denominators will divide into. The fractions ⅓, ⅕ and ⅙ have a lowest common denominator of 30. Their equivalent fractions are ¹⁰⁄₃₀, ⁶⁄₃₀ and ⁵⁄₃₀.

lowest common multiple See common multiple.

lowest terms To do with fractions being shown in their simplest form. This is done by cancelling as much as possible. ¹⁸⁄₂₄ shown in its lowest terms is ¾. Both parts of the fraction have been divided by 6.

m

mathematics The study of numbers, shapes, measures and position. It includes arithmetic.

method Way of doing something.

▲ Quarter of an hour is **less** time than half an hour.

$$3 \times 10 = 30$$
$$\frac{1}{3} = \frac{10}{30}$$

$$5 \times 6 = 30$$
$$\frac{1}{5} = \frac{6}{30}$$

$$6 \times 5 = 30$$
$$\frac{1}{6} = \frac{5}{30}$$

▲ The **lowest common denominator** of ⅓, ⅕ and ⅙ is 30.

million One thousand thousands. It is written as 1 000 000. The place where the 1 is, is called the millions place.

minus Subtract, or take away. The symbol - is often called the minus sign. (See also plus.)

minus number See negative number.

mixed fraction See mixed number.

mixed number Also called a mixed fraction. A number greater than 1 that is shown as a whole number and a fraction, such as 3½.

▲ 3½ is a **mixed number**.

multiple The numbers you say when you count on from a number in jumps of that number. The multiples of 2 are 2, 4, 6, 8, 10, 12 and so on. (See also common multiple.)

multiplication A number operation in which one number is multiplied by another.
4x3 means 4 multiplied by 3 , which is the same thing as three 4s or three lots of 4. It can be written as 4+4+4 which equals 12. So, multiplication can be thought of as repeated addition.
The order in which numbers are multiplied does not change the answer. 2x5=10 and 5x2=10.
Multiplication is the inverse of division. 15÷3=5, so 5x3=15. (See also product.)

▲ **Multiplication** can be used to find the number of buns on each tray.

multiplication tables

multiplication tables See times-tables.

multiply (multiplied) Make changes to a number using multiplication. The symbol for 'multiply by' is x.

negative number Also called a minus number. Any number less than, or below, zero. Negative numbers always have a minus sign written in front of them. The numbers -5, -86, -4.654, -5036 and -6¾ are all negative numbers.

non-commutative To do with the fact that the order of the numbers in subtraction and division operations cannot be changed. (See also commutative.)

none Not any. It is shown by the numeral 0. (See also zero.)

number Numbers represent amounts.

number facts Things that are true about numbers. Often linked to number operations. The addition facts of 5, for instance, are that it can be made by adding 0 and 5, 1 and 4, 2 and 3, 3 and 2, 4 and 1 or 5 and 0.

▲ On a snowy day it might be -4 degrees Celsius. -4 is a **negative number**.

$$0 + 5 = 5 \qquad 3 + 2 = 5$$
$$1 + 4 = 5 \qquad 4 + 1 = 5$$
$$2 + 3 = 5 \qquad 5 + 0 = 5$$

▲ These are the addition **number facts** of 5.

number line A line that has numbers marked on it in order. It is useful for working out simple number operations. (See also number track.)

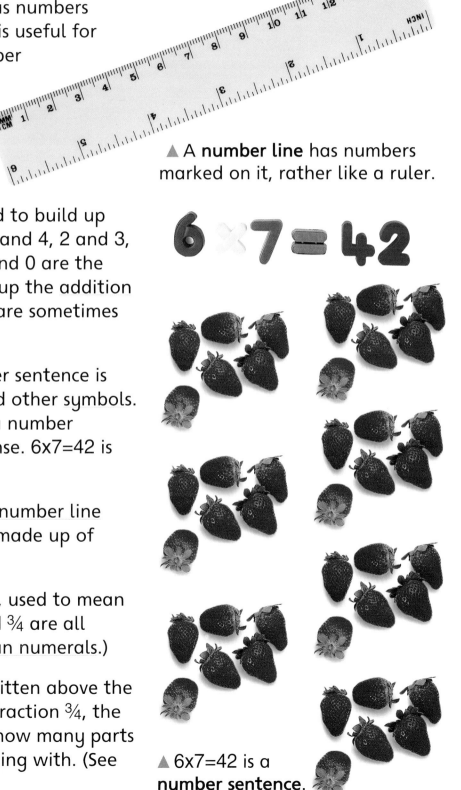

▲ A **number line** has numbers marked on it, rather like a ruler.

number pair Two numbers. Often linked to number operations. Pairs of numbers are used to build up number facts. 0 and 5, 1 and 4, 2 and 3, 3 and 2, 4 and 1 and 5 and 0 are the number pairs that make up the addition facts of 5. Number pairs are sometimes called number bonds.

number sentence A number sentence is made up of numerals and other symbols. Like a spoken sentence, a number sentence has to make sense. 6x7=42 is a number sentence.

number track Similar to a number line but, usually, like a path made up of separate sections.

numeral A symbol, or sign, used to mean a number. 4, 5·64, -8 and ¾ are all numerals. (See also Roman numerals.)

numerator The number written above the line in a fraction. In the fraction ¾, the numerator is 3. It shows how many parts of the whole we are dealing with. (See also denominator.)

▲ 6x7=42 is a **number sentence.**

odd

odd A whole number that cannot be divided exactly by 2. If you try to divide 5 by 2, you get two lots of 2 with an odd 1 left over. Any whole number that ends in 1, 3, 5, 7 or 9 is an odd number. The numbers 3, 47, 579 and 3645 are all examples of odd numbers. (See also even.)

one The number that means a single thing or amount. It is written as 1. Ones are also called units. (See also place and place value.)

one-to-one correspondence Match one thing with another. One-to-one correspondence can be used to compare two sets to find the difference. Counting is a form of one-to-one correspondence. Each object is matched with a number.

▲ These cups and saucers are matched in **one-to-one correspondence**.

operation To do with making changes to a number, using a set of rules. Addition, subtraction, multiplication and division are all number operations.

order To do with the way things follow on from each other. (See also ascending order and descending order.)

ordinal number Any number that describes order, for example, first, fifty-seventh or one hundred and sixty-fifth.

▲ The winner is the first in the race. First is an **ordinal number**.

p

pair Two. Or, match one thing up with another thing.

partition Separate. A set of beads, for example, can be partitioned, or separated, into different colours. The number 143 can be partitioned into 100, 40 and 3.

pattern To do with something being repeated or changed in the same way over and over again.
When counting in fives, for example, one number will end in 5, the next in 0, the next in 5, the next in 0 and so on. In the sequence 4, 8, 12, 16, 20, 24, 28, the pattern is a difference of four between each number.

percentage The number of parts in every hundred. It says how many hundredth parts of the whole something is. A percentage is a way of expressing a fraction. The phrase 'per cent' means 'out of one hundred'. The symbol for per cent is %. 5 hundredths (or 5 parts of something that has a hundred equal parts) is called 5 per cent and is written as 5%. 5% is equivalent to $\frac{5}{100}$.
100% is the whole of something because it means 100 parts out of something that has 100 equal parts.
50% is half of something. It means 50 parts out of 100 parts. 50 is half of 100.

▲ Two things can be called a **pair**.

▲ Exam results are often shown as a **percentage**.

place

place To do with the position of a digit within a number. In the number 3849, the 9 is in the ones, or units, place, the 4 is in the tens place, the 8 is in the hundreds place and the 3 is in the thousands place. (See also place value.)

place value Digits have different values depending on where they appear in a number. In the number 9457, the 7 has a value of 7 ones, or units, the 5 has a value of 5 tens, the 4 has a value of 4 hundreds and the 9 has a value of 9 thousands. (See also decimal place and place.)

plus Another word for add. The symbol + is often called the plus sign. (See also minus.)

positive number Any number greater than, or above, zero. The numbers 5, 86, 4·65, 5036 and 6¾ are all positive numbers.

predict Suggest what is going to happen or what an answer might be, usually by looking at what has already happened and seeing if it follows a rule or pattern.

prime factor A factor that is also a prime number. The factors of 14 are 1, 2, 4, 7 and 14. The prime factors are 2 and 7.

prime number Any number that is only divisible by 1 and itself. 7 is a prime number. It is only divisible by 1 and 7.

▲ The **place value** of a digit depends on where the digit is.

▲ 7 is a **prime number**.

product The answer reached by multiplying one number by another number. 5x3=15. 15 is the product.

proper fraction Also known as a vulgar fraction or a common fraction. A fraction with a numerator that is less than the denominator, for example ¾. (See also improper fraction.)

property To do with describing a number. The properties of 7, for example, include being an odd, prime number.

proportion To do with how much of the whole something is. If a row of beads follows a pattern of three red and then two blue, the proportion of red beads is three in five because three out of every five beads are red. It can be written as ⅗, 60% or 3:5. Proportion compares one part to the whole.

▲ The **proportion** of red buttons is two in every four buttons.

prove Show that something is true.

q

quarter One of four equal parts. It is a fraction. It is written as ¼ when expressed as a proper fraction. It is written as 25% when expressed as a percentage and 0·25 when expressed as a decimal fraction.
Four quarters make one whole.

▲ Each **quarter** of these juggling balls is a different colour.

quotient

quotient The number of times that one number can be divided into another number. 15÷5=3. 3 is the quotient.

r

ratio To do with comparing two amounts. A row of beads that follows a pattern of three red beads and then two blue beads has a ratio of three to two because there are three red beads for every two blue beads. It is usually written as 3:2.
Ratio compares two different parts of a whole.

reasonable Makes sense, or could be true.

recombine Put back together.

recurring Is repeated without end. In division, the answer sometimes ends with a recurring digit. The digit is usually written once, with a short line or dot above it.

reduce Make smaller or simpler. A fraction can be reduced by cancelling. (See also lowest terms.)

regroup Group in a different way. 20 can be regrouped as 1 ten and 10 units.

relationship The connection or pattern between things.

▲ The **ratio** of blue toothbrushes to orange toothbrushes is 1:2.

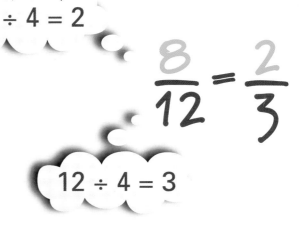

$$8 \div 4 = 2$$

$$\frac{8}{12} = \frac{2}{3}$$

$$12 \div 4 = 3$$

▲ This fraction has been **reduced** to its lowest terms.

remainder An amount that is left over. It often means the amount left over if one number cannot be divided by another number exactly. For instance, 13÷5=2 remainder 3.

repeated addition Adding a number to itself over and over again, for example 3+3+3+3=12. (See also multiplication.)

repeated subtraction Taking a number away from another number as many times as possible. 3 can be taken away from 12 four times. 12-3=9, 9-3=6, 6-3=3 and 3-3=0. (See also division.)

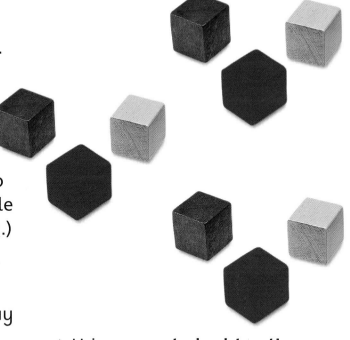

▲ Using **repeated subtraction**, 3 can be taken away from 9 three times.

represent Is a way of showing, or stand for.

Roman numerals A way of writing numbers that uses letters instead of digits. The letters LIX mean 59.

round Rounding a number to the nearest ten means finding the tens number that is closest to it.
32 rounded to the nearest ten is 30.
37 rounded to the nearest ten is 40.
35 is half-way between 30 and 40. All halfway numbers are rounded up, so 35 would be rounded up to 40.
Rounding is useful when estimating.

row A line that goes from side to side, rather than from top to bottom. (See also column.)

▲These birds are sitting in a **row**.

rule

rule A particular way of doing something or a pattern that is followed.

S

scale (scaling) Make bigger or smaller a certain number of times. You can think of multiplication as one number scaled up a particular number of times.

sequence A set of numbers or objects that are in order and which usually follow a pattern or rule.

set A group of things. The things often belong together in some way.

share (sharing) Give everyone or everything an equal amount.

solution The answer.

solve (solving) Find the answer.

sort Group for a particular reason.

square To find the square of a number, you multiply it by itself. 4x4=16, so 16 is 4 squared. It can be written as 4^2. A number, such as 16, which is another number squared is called a square number.

strategy Plan. How you decide to do something.

▲ The number **sequence** 3, 2, 1 has formed this pattern.

▲ This is a **set** of vegetables.

subtract Take away from. The symbol - is used to mean subtract. So, 6-3 means take 3 away from 6. (See also minus and subtraction.)

subtraction A number operation. Subtraction can be thought of as taking one number away from another number to find out how many are left. It can also be thought of as comparing two sets to find the difference between them or as finding how many have to be added to the second number to get to the first number.
The order of the numbers cannot be changed. 5-4 is not the same as 4-5. Subtraction is the inverse of addition. If 2+3=5 then 5-3=2. (See also minus.)

▲ This woman is taking, or **subtracting**, an apple from the shelf.

sum The answer you get when two or more numbers are added. The sum of 4 and 3 is 7.

symbol A sign that represents something, especially an idea. For example, the idea of multiplying one number by another number is shown by the symbol x.

tally Match up an object with a mark. It is a way of counting. Tally marks are usually drawn as groups of five lines.

▲ The **sum** of 4 and 3 is 7.

'teens' number

'teens' number Any of the numbers from 10 to 19.

ten Ten ones, or units. It is written as 10. The place where the 1 is, is called the tens place. Numbers like 10, 20, 30 and 40 are multiples of ten. They are sometimes called tens numbers. If something is divided into ten equal parts, each part is called a tenth.

third One of three equal parts. It is a fraction. It is written as ⅓ when expressed as a proper fraction. Three thirds make one whole.

thousand Ten hundreds. It is written as 1000. The place where the 1 is, is called the thousands place. If something is divided into one thousand equal parts, each part is called a thousandth.

times Multiplied by.

times-tables Also called multiplication tables. Multiplication facts that are arranged in lists. Each list is made up of numbers multiplied by one particular number, together with their products.

top-heavy fraction See improper fraction.

total How many there are or how much there is altogether. (See also sum.)

▲ Each **third** of this flag is a different colour.

▼ There are **thousands** of hairs on this girl's head.

unit One thing.

value How much something is worth or what amount it represents.

vulgar fraction See proper fraction.

whole All of something. One whole can be divided into parts, called fractions.

▲ Here is a **whole** cabbage.

whole number Any number that does not include a fraction. It can be positive or negative. 2, 4586, -4, -756 and 65 are all whole numbers. (See also integer.)

x
y
z

zero The number name for none. It is written as 0.
Although there are no tens in the number 101, the zero is needed to mark, or hold, the tens place. There are no whole numbers in the decimal fraction 0·492, but a zero is needed to mark the ones place.

▲ There are five eggs in this nest. Five is a **whole number**.

Index

The numbers that are printed in **bold** show the pages of the main explanations.
The numbers that are printed in *italics* show the pages where there are pictures.

A word may appear in more than one explanation on any one page.